Diesel Dining
The Art of Manifold Cooking

Cecil Jorgensen and Kathleen Szalay

Publication Consultants
Since 1978

PO Box 221974 Anchorage, Alaska 99522-1974
books@publicationconsultants.com
www.publicationconsultants.com

ISBN 978-1-59433-126-8
ebook 978-1-59433-139-8
Library of Congress Catalog Card Number: 2010921585

Manufactured in the United States of America.

Dedication

This book was inspired by Lindy Joyce Jorgensen
and we followed her dream to completion.

Diesel Dining: The Art of Manifold Cooking, is dedicated to
Cecil Jorgensen Sr.. The inspiration for this book came from
the family stories told by him from Loon Lake, Washington.
He recanted how his relatives Great Uncle Johnny and Har-
old Hagen from Fargo, North Dakota cooked chicken on the
manifold of their late model T in the 1920s as they ventured
out to the great northwest.

Disclaimer

The information in this cookbook reflects the authors' experiences and opinions regarding cooking on the manifold of a diesel engine semi truck. All material included in this publication is believed to be accurate.

This cookbook is for both cooking instruction and entertainment purposes, and how the authors electively chose to use their diesel engine as a cooking device. If you decide to try any of the recipes, you do so at your own risk. The same precautions in operating a semi truck and working under the hood apply when using the manifold as a cooking device. Care and common sense must prevail when working with heated elements, just as such prudence would be exercised when working with a traditional electric oven or stove. The publisher assumes no responsibility for any health, welfare, or subsequent damage that might be incurred from the use of these materials.

Warning: As with all other special precautions that apply to hauling hazardous materials, never use your truck's diesel engine as a cooking device when under a HAZMAT load.

Acknowledgments

The late, Carole Lowell Bendz Davis, published author, teacher, and writer served as an invaluable resource for *Diesel Dinning: The Art of Manifold Cooking.*

A special acknowledgement to John Russell Davis, whose telltale inherited quick whit, dry humor, and adventurous spirit are woven throughout the writings of this book. The world misses you, John.

To both of our family members and friends for their ongoing support, advise, encouragement, and words of wisdom. And a special recognition to Janet VanHorn, for providing a lot of fodder for this book.

To the entire staff, especially Tony and Dirk, at National Transportation Driver Training Centers in Spokane, Washington.

Table of Contents

Welcome

Welcome to *Diesel Dining: The Art of Manifold Cooking*. If you're a long haul trucker, and you want to enjoy a home-cooked, hot, meat and potatoes dinner at the end of your day's drive, then this is the one and only cookbook you'll ever need. You'll never see this cookbook in a typical homemaker's kitchen, since its premise is based on using your truck's diesel engine to cook your meals. Soon, this book will be dog-eared and stained with a variety of sauces, as it sits within easy reach by your interstate maps and daily log book.

All of these recipes were cooked on a 2001 Freightliner Classic XL with a 500 horsepower Detroit Diesel engine. Cooking times and distances vary depending on your rig and driving style.

To convince yourself that this book is worth using on a daily basis, and to verify the authenticity of your engine's cooking ability, invest twenty-five cents by purchasing one potato and one small onion. Wrap them in foil and place them on your manifold. Drive 200 miles and stop to wash your windshield, and take a deep breath. Aromatherapy at its finest—one hot baked potato and roasted onion to snack on when you take a break to peruse the myriad of diesel dining recipes found later in this book.

·

Diesel Dining Basics

What follows is the *meat and potatoes* basic recipe for this cookbook. The bulk of this cookbook offers a variety of recipes you can try cooking on your manifold. It also includes tips, tricks, stories, and trucking folklore. But if your intention is to start cooking in a hurry and get back to the business of truck driving, the recipe below uses the most fundamental items needed to cook on your truck's Detroit Diesel engine.

Old School Cooking
The Only Recipe You Really Need

Meat
Potatoes and onions (optional)
Tin foil
Pocket knife

Use your pocket knife to cut the potato and onion into pieces. Wrap in foil with meat, place on manifold, and drive 400 miles.

Why You Need *Diesel Dining:*
The Art of Manifold Cooking

Quite simply, you need this cookbook if:
• You are tired of eating greasy fast food.
• You are more often than not economically challenged, and fed up with trading your hard-earned cents per mile for overpriced junk food. This includes buying antacids such as Rolaids, necessary to overcome eating the grease and grit found in most commercially available food products.
• You don't have access to cooking appliances, or have been holding off purchasing one of the many cooking gadgets available that plug into a vehicle's cigarette lighter. Using the methods in this cookbook, there is no kitchen required. No oven, no microwave, no devices that can break after one or two uses, and no electricity—just draw on the diesel power you're already using to drive your truck and earn your living. In fact, there is no cost but the bare necessities and the food itself.
• The mere act of meal preparation, and enjoying the culinary results of your efforts, is a relaxing and effortless task to both the start and end your driving day. You can unwind and dine at the same time.
• This idea is too good not to be shared with the hundreds of

thousands of truck drivers on the road—an industry that offers job security and is growing on an annual basis. This cookbook is a solution to keeping more money in your pocket, eating delicious meat and potatoes dishes that cost less than 1/10th of what you'd pay for one fast food meal, and having fun doing it.

- Eating has always been a social event, and life on the road is lonely. Now you can pull into a truck stop, check your oil, and meet new friends when the savory smell of onions and meat is wafting from your diesel engine.
- As a bonus, this book's a fun read and conversation topic. It makes a perfect and well-appreciated gift for a wanderlust friend or relative that most everyone has in their family tree.

What You Won't Find In This Cookbook

It is not the intention of this cookbook to tell you how to live or what to eat. You have gotten by this far, and just the fact that you're reading this now is proof you've done a great job of it. The recipes in this cookbook do not count calories, include charts that assign *point values* used by trendy weight loss programs, or suggest alternate ingredients (such as reducing sugar or carbohydrate intake) for those going through a fad diet phase. If this information is essential to your health, seek the advice of your doctor or a qualified nutritionists.

There are also certain cookbooks supposedly written with the truck driver in mind. They are so sugar coated and prissy you almost lose your meal just reading the flowery story that precedes each recipe. The authors of this authentic trucker's cookbook you are reading would never name names, but a picture is worth a thousand words ….

This cookbook is for truck drivers that are hungry. Hard working people that don't have the luxury of being at home, and want something at the end of a long day that resembles a home cooked dinner. This cookbook teaches you how to prepare good, healthy, hot, affordable meals. It is guaranteed to save you thousands of dollars a year by removing the temptation and impulse buying of overpriced fast food products when you are famished and too exhausted to cook.

Chapter 1
Where's the Beef?

Beef is what a real man wants for dinner. Being the last American Cowboy, there is no need for going out on the range and roping your own steer. But you can sure cook up a lot of good grub using the diesel engine of your iron horse. The recipes in this chapter will satisfy the appetite of even the hungriest trucker's craving for meat.

Basic Beef

This recipe is guaranteed, tried, and true. It will become one of your staple meals for either lunch or dinner.

> 1 pound bottom round roast
> 2 medium potatoes
> 1 small onion, chopped
> Chopped pieces of carrot and celery

Dice potatoes, or leave whole and pierce. Place above ingredients in cooking pan sealed with foil. Place securely on manifold. Drive 500 miles at 60 to 65 mph. Serve with warmed and seasoned vegetables of your choice. The total cost of this meal is equivalent to driving 30 miles.

18-Wheel Value Meal

Forget those fast food "value meal" temptations. When you order a burger at a well known, burger chain it cost you more than $6? At .25 cents a mile, that's 24 miles you have to drive. You can enjoy our value meal, and it's a roast to boot, for an average cost of .13 cents a serving (that's only ½ mile of driving time to you).

> 1 beef bottom round roast
> 2 tablespoons flour
> 2 teaspoons salt
> ¼ cup oil or lard
> 2 cups water

Place all ingredients in cooking tin, cover with foil, and complete your day's drive. When you're through, enjoy the savory taste of this less-inexpensive cut off meat which will slice with a butter knife it's so tender.

New England Pot Roast

Some drivers don't enjoy driving the Eastern states. If your dispatcher sends you there anyway, at least your consolation prize will be this hardy dinner.

> 1 to 2 pound roast (the cheaper, the better)
> Dijon mustard
> Onions
> Carrots
> Celery
> Potatoes
> Gravy mix

After picking up a morning load in New England, spread top of roast with mustard after placing in cooking tin with chopped onions and halved potatoes. Cover entire dish with gravy, and seal tightly using high quality aluminum foil. Place on manifold; by the time you unload (450 miles) you'll be able to kick back and enjoy a complete diesel-cooked roast dinner.

Trucker's Tangerine Beef

4 tangerines or 3 medium navel oranges, peeled
    and diced
1 boneless beef top sirloin steak
3 tablespoons oil or lard
2 tablespoons corn starch
1 large piece of broccoli, cut into bite size pieces
2 tablespoons water
1 chopped red bell pepper
3 green onions, chopped fine
3 garlic cloves, minced
1 tablespoon ginger
3 packages of soy sauce
½ teaspoon crushed red pepper

Place all ingredients in strong cooking tin and cover with foil.
Drive 525 miles before serving.

Diesel Barbecued Spareribs

4-6 pounds pork spareribs, cut into two-rib portions
1 can tomato paste
½ cup water
½ cup vinegar
¼ cup honey
½ cup brown sugar
2 tablespoons oil
Chopped onions
2 teaspoons salt
2 teaspoons chili powder

Arrange spareribs in single layer on long cooking tin. Blend together remaining ingredients and pour over ribs, rotating a few times to coat. Place on manifold, covered with foil, for 435 miles.

Missouri Meatloaf

This is a home cooked meal that grandmother would be proud of!

1/8th pound ground round
Chopped onions
2 packets of catsup
Splash of Worchester sauce
Bread crumbs
Salt and pepper

Mix above ingredients. Pack into cleaned soup can with both ends removed, and then cover each end with foil. Poke a couple of small wholes for drainage, and place end down on manifold. Rotate can from end-to-end every 150 miles for 600 miles.

Tip: *When serving, save the ends of the soup can. Use one of the lids to push out the meatloaf slice to the desired width, then use the other end to slice off a portion. Arrange on a paper plate with brown gravy (page 83), and be sure to round out the meal with potatoes and vegetables.*

HOS Hobo Stew

Because of the January 4th, 2004 change in the HOS rules (assuming the rules are still in effect as of the printing of this book), you need to drive longer to cook this stew (and, of course, you're earning less, so buy the cheapest cut of meat you can find).

> 1 cheap cut of beef
> 1 potato
> ½ cup water
> Brown gravy (on page 83)
> Dice potato.

Place above ingredients in cooking pan sealed with foil. Place securely on manifold. Bake for 10 hours at 60 to 65 mph.

Bonus Pay Beef Tenderloin

As a trucker, you work long hard hours. Every so often, you need to treat yourself to the best cut of meat available. Toss this dish on your engine when you get a few extra dollars in your next paycheck.

2 pound beef tenderloin
2 tablespoons grape juice
1 tablespoon chopped tarragon
1 tablespoon vinegar
2 tablespoons orange juice
1/2 cup butter

Place beef, fat side up, in sturdy metal tin (you don't want to risk this dish spilling out into your engine). Mix remaining ingredients, and smear on top of beef. Cover with high quality aluminum foil, and cook slowly on manifold for 350 miles (rare).

Where's the Beef
Rib Roast with Baked Patatoe

1 beef rib roast
Salt and pepper to taste
Large patatoe

Place beef, fat side up, in shallow tin pan. Sprinkle with salt and pepper. Do not add water. Roast lightly covered on manifold for 400 to 600 miles, depending on desired degree of doneness (use your meat thermometer): 135ºF (rare), 23 to 25 minutes per pound; 155ºF (medium), 27 to 30 minutes per pound.

Thirty minutes before beef reaches desired temperature, remove beef dish from manifold. Spoon off drippings from roasting pan to measure 2 tablespoons and place back in pan. Bake another 100 miles. Keep the dish covered with tent of aluminum foil and let stand for 30 minutes.

Glazed Meatballs and Noodles

½ pound hamburger
¼ spoon cornstarch
10 packets grape jelly
Cooking bag and cooking foil tray

Form hamburger into meatballs the size of ping-pong balls, place into an aluminum cooking pan, and seal with foil. Cook for 400 miles at 1500 rpm. Mix cornstarch and grape jelly well, and spoon mixture over cooked meatballs (without draining the drippings from the bottom of the pan). Reseal and bake for an additional 100 miles. The jelly mixture crystallizes the meat, and these are a surprisingly delicious dish.

Manifold-Cooked Beef

Tortillas
Rice
Cheese
Two beef bouillon cubes

Take two tortillas, position the beef pieces in a line a little off center, and wrap the burritos. A good trick for wrapping burritos tightly is to first fold the tortilla over two edges around an inch. Hold the folded edges with your pinkies, and use your thumbs to roll and simultaneously press and seal the ingredients into the tortilla (this is the same technique you use to tightly wrap and turn a bed roll or sleeping bag).

Place the burritos in a pan coated with cooking spray. Dissolve two beef bouillon cubes in water, and add to pan with one cup of minute rice. Seal and bake for four hours, adding shredded or sliced cheese the last hour.

BBQ Ribs

Rack of beef ribs
Barbecue sauce (page 75)

Put ribs in large cooking tin, and douse thoroughly with barbecue sauce. Place on manifold and cook the entire day, or for 600 miles at 60 mph. Stir and flip ribs each time you stop for fuel or to use the facilities.

Pineapple Roasted Rib

Rack of beef ribs
1 can pineapple chunks
1 tablespoon brown sugar
1 package soy sauce
2 cloves

Stick the cloves into the ribs, place meat in large cooking tin, and cover with remaining ingredients. Place on manifold and cook for 475 miles at 65 to 70 mph.

Margarita Steak

2 boneless beef strips
¾ teaspoon salt
¼ teaspoon cayenne pepper
1 teaspoon cumin
1 tablespoon oil or lard
2 red onions, sliced
1 lime
2 tablespoons orange juice
1 can chicken broth
¼ cup cilantro, chopped
1 avocado, peeled and sliced

Place all ingredients except avocado in sturdy baking tin, cover with foil, and cook on manifold for 625 miles. WARNING: This dish smells absolutely delicious while you're driving: remember to open the air vents in your tractor every once in a while to take a whiff. Serve the steak dinner topped with avocado slices. For at-home-cooking, this dish goes nicely with a frosty Margarita and lime.

Shiska-bobtails

Stew size cuts of meat
Onion
Fresh, small white mushrooms
Bell pepper (red and yellow)
Cherry tomatoes

Chop vegetables (except for mushrooms) into large, bite size pieces. Arrange items on skewers in alternating sequence. Lay skewers in rectangular tin, cover with foil, and cook on manifold for 450 miles at 1200 rpm.

Eat More Chicken Beef Stew

For the cow's version of this recipe, see page 41.

1 pound beef stew meat, cut into 1/2-inch pieces
1 medium onion, chopped (1/2 cup)
Potatoes, cut into fourths
1 bag (8 ounces) baby-cut carrots
1 can Vegall* large cut vegetables
1 can (10 1/2 ounces) condensed beef broth
3 tablespoons flour
Water
Salt and pepper

Place meat in a plastic bag and add flour, salt, and pepper. Shake well to coat the meat with the flour mixture, and empty into a tin foil baking pan. Peel and dice the onion, potato, and carrot. Drain the canned vegetables, and add all remaining ingredients to the beef in the cooking pan. Cover with in 2 to 3 cups of water and seal tightly with tin foil. Place on manifold, and cook for 8 to 10 hours at 60 mph.

Curds and Weigh Station Stew

Beef round steak
2 tablespoons bacon fat
1 large onion, sliced
Sliced mushrooms
2 tablespoons flour
1 teaspoon salt
Pinch of dried thyme and marjoram leaves
1/8 teaspoon pepper
1/2 cup beef bouillon
  1 cup red wine or tomato juice (if you cannot use
    either of these, use apple juice instead)

Cut beef into 1-inch cubes. Place into foil cooking pan with remaining ingredients. Cover tightly and cook on manifold 600 miles. Check on beef at a fuel stop: If necessary, stir in additional bouillon and wine (1 part bouillon to 2 parts wine).

Truck Stop Teriyaki

1 pound sirloin steak
Teriyaki sauce (page 82)
Small onion
1 can crushed pineapple

Cut sirloin into 1 inch strips, place in foil cooking pan, add crushed pineapple, teriyaki sauce, and onions. Seal with foil and slow cook on manifold for 5 hours under load or overnight on idle (add one cup water to mix for overnight cooking)

Mardi Gras Manifold Madness

This recipe is actually the trucker's rendition of the classic beef stroganoff, cooked while cruising through New Orleans.

> 1 pound lean ground beef
> 1/3 cup chopped onion
> 1 package (3/4 ounce) mushroom gravy mix
> 3/4 cup water
> 1 jar (2 1/2 ounces) sliced mushrooms, drained
> 1 cup sour cream
> 1 cup Original Bisquick® mix
> 1/4 cup milk
> 1 egg
> 1 small bell pepper, cut into rings

Grease tin pan. Mix beef, onion, gravy mix (dry), water, mushrooms, and sour cream and spoon mixture into pan. Stir Bisquick mix, milk and egg until blended. Spread evenly over beef mixture. Top with bell pepper rings.

Place on manifold, covered tightly with foil, and drive 425 miles. Let stand 15 minutes after removing from engine and cutting.

Little Italy Lasagna

Fresh lasagna noodles
Tomato sauce
Ricotta or cottage cheese
1 egg (if available)
Parsley

Place the noodles in a long, rectangular tin pan and cover with water. Seal the pan tightly with foil, and bake overnight at 900 rpm.

In the morning, drain the water from the noodles and reuse the pan. Alternately layer the cooked noodles, tomato sauce (canned or homemade; see page 80), and cheese. Sprinkle chopped parsley on top of the dish, seal with foil, and bake at 60 mph for 8 hours.

This lasagna is so darn good, it is worth making a very large batch and snacking on leftovers for the entire week.

Kielbasa Supper Skillet

1 hunk of kielbasa
Head of cabbage
2 potatoes
1 onion
¾ cup water
Pinch of parsley
Salt and pepper

Chop kielbasa into bite size chunks. Shred the cabbage, chop the potatoes and onions, and place this and all remaining ingredients into metal foil pan. Cover with foil, poke 2-3 times for the steam to escape, and place on the manifold. Drive for your supper skillet dinner around 400 miles.

Bacon-Wrapped Beef (Land Runnin' Pigs)

Any cut of boneless beef
Pepper bacon

Cut meat into long strips. Lay each strip on a piece of pepper bacon and roll: use a toothpick to secure. Place in baking tin covered with foil on manifold, and cook for 325 miles. These are both great as a snack or a main dish served with potatoes and vegetables.

Chapter 2
Chicken and Poultry

The "Eat More Chicken" billboards found throughout the United States are some of our favorites ... for a recipe where the ruffled fowls get their revenge, see page 36.

Coffee Can Chicken

The preparation of this chicken is what gives it such a moist, delicious flavor.

> Small chicken
> Soda can
> Large clean coffee can

Fill soda can with with water or any beverage. Place the can inside chicken cavity and put both into the large coffee can,seal with foil. Place on manifold and cook under load for 550 miles or 10 hours @1100 rpm. Check for doneness using a meat thermometer.

Tin Can Chicken in a Coffee Can

One whole chicken
Small onion
1 cube chicken bouillon

Wash chicken thoroughly. Remove the chicken wings (never eat anything called "wings" from a bird that cannot fly). Place onion and bouillon cube in soup or tin can full of water, cover, and idle on manifold for 30 miles to boil. Put chicken in coffee can and cover with bouillon sauce. Cover and cook on manifold for 11 hours at 65 mph.

Crispy Corn Flake Chicken

1 pound boneless, skinless chicken breasts
One 12-ounce fountain cup of corn flakes cereal

For an Italian herb coating, use:
1 spoonful dried basil flakes
1 spoonful dried oregano
½ teaspoon garlic powder
Dash of pepper

For a Mexican herb coating, use:
1 spoonful chili powder
½ teaspoon cumin
½ teaspoon garlic powder
Dash of black pepper
Dash of red pepper

Put corn flakes in plastic bag and crush to crumble. Add the chicken and one of the herb coatings above into the plastic bag, and shake well.

Put chicken pieces into a foil baking pan sprayed with cooking oil. Cover and cook on manifold for 450 miles.

Coeur d'Alene Chicken Cordon Blue

2 boned, skinless chicken breasts
2 slices ham
2 slices Swiss cheese
1 cup bread crumbs
1 tablespoon cooking oil
Chopped parsley
2 tablespoons flour

Butterfly chicken breasts and layer with ham and cheese. Roll each one burrito-style. Coat with flour, then drizzle with oil before rolling in bread crumbs. Put chicken in a tin pan, sprinkle with parsley, and cover with foil. Place on manifold and drive until juices run clear, around 500 miles.

Green Onion Chicken Burritos

Canned chicken
Tortillas
Rice
Cheese
1 can cream of chicken soup

Take two tortillas, sprinkle the shredded chicken in a line a little off center, and wrap the burritos. A good trick for wrapping burritos tightly is to first fold the tortilla over two edges around an inch. Hold the folded edges with your pinkies, and use your thumbs to roll and simultaneously press and seal the ingredients into the tortilla (this is the same technique you use to tightly wrap and turn a bed roll or sleeping bag).

Place the burritos in a pan coasted with cooking spray. Pour in a can of creamed chicken soup and one cup of minute rice. Seal and bake for four hours, adding shredded or sliced cheese the last hour.

Route 66 Drumsticks

These drumsticks will really keep you rolling, as you cruise down Route 66.

>1 package chicken drumsticks
>Mop sauce (page 77)
>Flour

Coat drumsticks in chixen rub, place in sturdy metal tin, and cover with mop sauce. Cover with foil and bake for 500 miles.

Chicken and Dumplings

Chicken and dumplings are a staple defining a good, old fashioned, home cooked meal. The basics include chicken and gravy, and mushrooms and vegetables. The "dumpling" portion can be store bought homemade broiled biscuits (using the Sourdough Starter dough on page 70), Pillsbury biscuits, fresh noodles, or wide flat pasta noodles.

> Chicken
> Onion
> Poultry seasoning
> Salt and pepper
> Carrots
> Celery
> Flour

Remove the skin from a boneless chicken (ever wonder how a chicken walks with no bones?), rinse thoroughly, and cut into bite size pieces. Chop a medium onion, and 1 ½ cup each of carrots and celery. Mix a ½ cup of flour with 3 cups of water. Place all ingredients in a tin roasting pan, and add poultry seasoning, salt, and pepper to taste. Cover with foil and drive until the chicken is fork tender and the gravy is thickened, around 400 to 500 miles.

Serve in a heavy-duty plastic bowl, covered with dumplings (see page 74), sourdough biscuits, or prepared Pillsbury biscuits.

Chapter 3
Porkin' Out

Maple-Glazed Smoked Pork

1 healthy pat of butter
2 packets (tablespoons) maple syrup
1 packet (teaspoon) mustard
Pinch ground red pepper
2 splashed of bourbon (optional)
4 chops of boneless smoked pork

Melt butter in tin can on pre-heated engine. Add maple syrup, mustard (using Dijon tastes the best), and red pepper. Swirl and drive 25 miles.

Transfer to tin baking dish and add some bourbon if desired (never to be stored on your rig: even if the seal hasn't been broken). Stir in pork slices and return to manifold, covered with aluminum foil. Turn at each rest or fuel stop until meat is deeply glazed (around 300 to 350 miles).

Chapter 4
Goin' Fishing

Oysters Rockefeller

Since oysters are a well known aphrodisiac, they are best enjoyed in the company of your favorite rider.

Fresh oysters
Tabasco
Fresh lemon
Garlic salt

Using a pocketknife, slice open oysters and clean thoroughly. Place the oyster meat back onto the half shell.

Serve the oysters with a salty dipping sauce by mixing together diesel-roasted peanuts (following the recipe on page 93), garlic, salt, lemon, and Tabasco sauce.

Chapter 5
Cookin' with Spuds

After cleaning potatoes, rub skin with oil or lard. And always poke holes in whole potatoes to allow the steam to escape. As a general rule of thumb, potatoes are always baked to perfection in 300 miles (regardless of road conditions, speed, grade, or engine size).

Baked Potatoes

Large russet potatoes
Butter

Coat washed potato skins with butter, poke with holes, and double wrap in foil. Place on manifold, and bake for 300 miles at 60 mph.

Port of Entry Potatoes (Jo Jo's)

Two potatoes
Onion
Cooking oil
Parmesan cheese
Parsley (fresh or dried flakes)
Seasoning salt

Slice potatoes into long strips, cut the onion into good-sized chunks, and place in paper sack with remaining ingredients. Shake the mixture hard, coating the potatoes well, and pour onto a piece of tin foil. Wrap and twist the foil at both ends, and bake on the manifold from Seattle, Washington to the Oregon Port of Entry station, or approximately 250 miles.

Chapter 6
Beans and Other Vegetables

When diesel cooking your vegetable, always use the highest (i.e., strongest) quality aluminum foil.

Baked Onions

Nothing provides more stimulating aromatherapy as you're driving while your dinner cooks and you smell baked onions wafting from the engine manifold though the truck's air vents …

> One whole onion
> Butter (optional)

Wrap an onion tightly in aluminum foil–do not peel the onion prior to wrapping. Prior to doing this, you can optionally slit the top of the onion and dab in a generous helping of butter. Place on the manifold and bake for 300 miles. Of course, accompany the onion with one of your favorite manifold meat recipes.

Sweet, white onions work best because their shells leaves a nice, browned coating when done.

Fresh Asparagus in a Can

Webster's dictionary defines the word oxymoron as "a figure of speech in which apparently contradictory terms appear in conjunction (e.g., faith unfaithful kept him falsely true)."

Does this recipe title sound like an oxymoron? Well, it is! But the taste is too good to stigmatize with such a fittingly descriptive adjective… just follow the instructions and enjoy!

Ripened stalks of fresh asparagus
Butter (NOT optional)

Clean the asparagus, and snap off the ends. The trick to know where to snap an asparagus is to shuffle the stalk through your hands and test at occasional points to see where an easy break naturally occurs. Let the vegetable be your guide—no knives are needed.

Place the spears upright (woody side down) in a tin soup can. Add a healthy slab of butter and cover tightly with foil before placing on manifold. Bake at 200 miles. If desired, wrap cooked asparagus in foil and place back on manifold for another 100 miles to sear and brown the outside of the vegetables.

Food tip: *You can substitute green beans for the asparagus, or any fresh vegetable for that matter.*

Air Horn Corn on the Cob

2 fresh ears of corn
Butter

Wrap corn cobs tightly in foil, twisting both ends securely closed. Place on manifold and cook for 350 miles. Season with butter, salt, and pepper to taste.

Stuffed Bell Peppers

2 large green bell peppers
Cooked ground beef
Minute rice
Tomato sauce
Onions
Salt and pepper

Chop one end off the bell pepper, and clean out the seeds. Mix remaining ingredients, stuff into peppers, and double wrap with foil. Bake on manifold for 350 miles at 55 mph.

Boston to Philly Baked Beans and Rice

1 tablespoon oil
Chopped carrot and celery pieces
Large diced onion
3 crushed garlic cloves
1 packet of salt
¾ cup long-grain rice
1 ½ cups water
1 big tablespoon Louisiana-style cayenne pepper sauce
2 large cans of black beans
Chopped cilantro

Mix all ingredients together into a tin pan. Cover and bake on manifold from Boston, MA to Philadelphia, PA (or the equivalent of 304 miles. Traveling West for proper cooking is not necessary.

Chapter 7
Salads, Soups, and Sandwiches

Trucker Chili con Carne

Chili con Carne is a favorite and filling dish of all truckers. If you have a rider on board, you might want some Beano for dessert!

> ½ pound ground beef
> ½ envelope chili flavored mix
> Kidney beans (one can)
> Onion
> Salt, pepper, and garlic salt

Dice a small onion, and mix with ground beef in a tin pan. Add remaining ingredients and pour in ½ cup of water. Stir, cover tightly with foil, and cook on manifold for 450 miles.

When serving, top chili with chopped tomatoes and shredded cheese. Crush a bunch of saltine crackers and sprinkle them onto of your diesel cooked chili con carne creation.

Coleslaw

Coleslaw, aside from being an excellent source of fiber, is a perfect accompaniment to meat dishes such as BBQ ribs (page 32) or Sloppy Joe sandwiches. Coleslaw found in deli sections across the U.S.A. is most often mass-produced, and is either too wet, sweet or spicy, which overpowers the flavor of the rest of the meal. Following is the basic recipe for 'slaw—without all the frills. Toss in any of the optional ingredients, doctoring up the salad depending on your palette.

Cabbage
1 cup mayonnaise
2 packets mustard
Sugar
1 tablespoon pickle juice
Dell pickle or sweet relish (10 packages, or ½ a cup)
Optional:
Purple cabbage (shredded)
Honey mustard
Raisins
Nuts

How much cabbage you need depends on your preference. For large chunks, chop 3 cups. For long strips of cabbage, shred 2 cups, or finely chop 1 cup. Add above ingredients to the chopped cabbage, seal the container tightly, and refrigerate overnight. The next day, stir well and serve. Coleslaw gets better with time as the flavors combine and absorb into the density of the ruffage.

Broccolini Salad with Red Peppers and Onions

Broccolini is a cross between broccoli and Chinese kale—it tastes like broccoli blended with asparagus. This is one of the yuppier recipes in this trucking cookbook: if you've never had broccolini before, try it and impress your trucking compadres with your culinary talents!

> 1 pound broccolini
> Onion
> Red bell pepper
> 2 tablespoons olive oil
> 2 teaspoons balsamic vinegar
> 1 pinch salt
> Freshly ground black pepper

Chop the broccolini into bite size pieces: the entire stalk is edible. If you cannot find this vegetable, substitute broccoli florets. Finely dice half the onion. Clean the seeds from the washed bell pepper, and cut into long shredded pieces. Place vegetables in cooking tin pan, add a splash of water, and cover tightly with foil poking a few holes on top. Steam on the manifold for 100 miles.

Arrange the steamed, roasted vegetables on a plate. Whisk together oil, vinegar, salt, and ground pepper to taste. Pour over salad, and top with a shake or two of dried parmesan-romano cheese.

BBQ Beef Sandwich

Use either leftover beef for this finger licking good sandwich, or cook a fresh hunk of meat from scratch.

> ½ pound thick sliced beef
> Sliced onion
> BBQ sauce
> Kaiser roll

Put above ingredients in cooking pan sealed with foil, placing sliced onions on top. Roast for 200 miles on manifold at 1600 rpm.

Hint: Warm large rolls last 200 miles (a Kaiser roll is recommended since it is firm and won't fall apart under the weight of the meat and sauce). Assemble sandwiches, kick back by an open campfire with a cup of Cowboy Coffee (page 103), and peruse your favorite trucking magazine. Or better yet, read this cookbook!

Hot Beef Sandwich

Cooked beef
Brown gravy (page 83)

Slather sliced hunks of meat between two pieces of your favorite bread, and pile high with gravy. Eat, then retire to your sleeper berth for 8 hours to digest this delicious meal.

Mile Marker Meatball Sandwich

Meatballs (use leftovers; see page 30)
One small onion
Hoagie rolls
Mozzarella cheese

Using the same aluminum foil pan you used to store them in, warm the leftover meatballs on the manifold for 250 miles. Wrap the rolls in aluminum foil, and place on manifold for toasting last 100 miles. Build the sandwich (use a sturdy plate!), and pile high with chopped onions and shredded mozzarella cheese. This sandwich is even better when served with a healthy portion of Jo Jo potatoes (page 54) and coleslaw (page 60).

Lebanon Baloney Sandwich

Next time you deliver a load on the East Coast, pick up a pound or two of Lebanon baloney. After consuming one of these delicacies, you'll never be tempted by commercial bologna again!

> 4 slices Lebanon baloney
> Sourdough bread
> Mustard
> Lettuce, tomatoes, and sliced red onions
> Pickle

Bake a loaf of sourdough bread, and slice off enough for sandwiches. Pile bread high with Lebanon baloney and mustard. Add lettuce, fresh tomatoes, and red onions. Serve sandwich with a thick kosher pickle slice and a generous helping of coleslaw (page 60) or cup of split pea soup (page 66).

Blister Bread (for sandwiches)

If you're not concerned with calories and the doc hasn't got you watching your daily cholesterol intake, serve any sandwich of your liking (hot or cold) on Blister Bread. Although you cannot make this bread on your manifold, the recipe is included for the welcome times you are at home and have the luxury of using an oven broiler.

> Sandwich rolls
> Real butter
> Lunch meat
> Fresh mozzarella cheese slices (buffalo milk
>   mozzarella is the best)
> Optional toppings (lettuce, olives, onions,
>   tomatoes, or pepperoncini)

Melt butter in microwave, slice fresh sandwich rolls in half, and place on broiling pan. Melt butter and drizzle evenly over rolls. Top with even layers of cheese slices, being sure to cover exposed area of bread.

Slide pan onto oven rack positioned halfway between the broiling element and the bottom of the oven. Flip oven control to Broil, and leave the oven door open a jar. After 5 minutes or so as the broiler becomes red hot, check on rolls. The blister bread is done when the white mozzarella cheese is a baked, blistered golden brown.

Carefully remove the hot bread slices, and smear on a thin layer of real mayonnaise. Add your favorite meat, and use your creativity. For example, use fresh deli ham and top with shredded lettuce, chopped olives, and tomatoes. Evenly pour some Italian dressing over the vegetables.

Wrap the entire sandwich roll in a large paper towel, and slice at a cross angle. Tuck one edge of the towel under the ½ sandwich's edge (to catch the drizzle) and take that first bite … blister bread at its finest! This bread is also excellent for making roast beef sandwiches; the bread and resultant sandwich is so sturdy, it won't fall apart when dipped in the hot au jus sauce.

Split Pea Soup

2 pats of butter
2 small leeks, picked fresh from the field
2 carrots
1 onion
½ cup celery
2 large, minced cloves of garlic
8 cups chicken broth
1 pound dried green split peas
2 ham hocks

Mix above ingredients in large coffee can, seal with foil and set on manifold over night at idle. Check liquid level the next morning and fill with water if low. Reseal with heavy duty foil and cook for 500 miles under load. Check liquid level every 100 miles and fill as necessary

Leek Soup

Bunch of leeks, picked fresh from the field (not the
    one you hit on the side of the road)
2 carrots
1 onion
½ cup celery
4 cups Cup 'O Chicken soup broth

Mix above ingredients and place in large coffee can,seal it
tight and simmer on manifold for 250 miles. Check liquid every 100 miles.

Navy Bean Soup

2 16-ounce cans of navy beans
2-3 ham hocks
1 cup chopped celery
1 cup chopped onion
Pinch of salt and pepper
Shake of Tabasco hot sauce
2 cups water

Place all ingredients in large foil tin, and bake on manifold for 600 miles. When preparing the soup, strip the ham meat from the bones; it should flake right off very easily.

Words of Wisdom Alphabet Soup

Words of wisdom: Never take a leak in a lightening storm.

1 package alphabet pasta
3 cups water
1 cup chopped celery
1 cup chopped onion
Salt and pepper

Place all ingredients in large foil tin, and bake on manifold for 300 miles. Read your dinner, and see if it spells out any answers or offers words of wisdom as to why you're working so hard for such low wages.

Chapter 8
Breakfast, Breads, and Muffins

Baking Bread: Making the Dough

There are a wide variety of breads you can make from scratch:

- Yeast breads
- Sourdough breads
- No rise breads

You can rise punched out bread dough while idling for an hour or two. If the state you are parked does not allow truck idling (as more are doing, such as New York), raise the dough while searching for a consignee's drop off address in a lower speed neighborhood.

While these simple recipes take a little bit of work, you can use the frozen stuff. But if you're feeling stressed and homesick, this is a good relaxing tool. This bread is considerably different, not only in the way you bake it in your engine, but because yeast is a living organism, and when you set it in your engine to get it to rise, the vibration drives it nuts and stimulates it to rise.

If you're delivering to any beer manufacturing plant in USA, ask if you can get a live yeast sample. Most brew masters will gladly provide you with a sample as long as they know you're not taking it to replicate their brew; they'll just think you're a bit odd because you want it to bake bread on your engine.

Sourdough Starter

Use this sourdough starter as the basis for making awesome tasting breads, pancakes, and biscuits.

> Plain yogurt
> 1 tablespoon flour

Put plain yogurt in a glass jar. Stir in flour, seal the jar tightly, and store in a dark place (for example, in the compartment under your lower sleeper berth) for one week to allow the mixture to bubble and ferment.

After a week's time, a clear liquid should have risen to the top of the sourdough starter mix—if the liquid is even remotely pinkish in hue, throw the entire batch out and start again (this is an indication that the bacteria in the yogurt has spoiled). Stir in the liquid, cover, and let sit for another week. Every couple of weeks, pour off half of the mixture and add 2 tablespoons of flour to keep building and regenerating the sourdough starter mix.

When you're ready to bake, take half of the sourdough starter mixture and place into a glass bowl. Add 2 to 3 tablespoons of flour, stir, and cover overnight. Then use the amount called for in your recipe.

Sponge Starter

Use the sponge starter mix when you have a package of yeast avail-able; this starter is good for making most all types of breads.

3 cups of flour
½ teaspoon active dry yeast

Put flour, yeast, and 1 1/3rd cup of warm water (105 to 115 degrees) in a bowl. Beat around three minutes, until batter is smooth and elastic. Scrape starter into larger bowl. Cover with plastic wrap, and keep cold for 15 to 24 hours.

Note: Starter is ready to use when the volume has tripled, it has thinned out slightly, and small bubbles appear on the surface. When starter is ready, let stand, covered, 30 minutes at room tem-perature before using.

Overnight Breakfast Sandwich

2 to 4 slices white bread
Butter
Ham
Cheese

Lightly butter the bread (using thick, white bread is recommended), and add meat and cheese to form sandwiches. Wrap each sandwich in foil, and place on manifold. Idle overnight.

Tip: If you have a BBQ on board and already have it fired up for making dinner (for example, barbecue steak), fry an egg real quick and add it to your breakfast sandwich.

Frozen Waffles

Use Eggos frozen waffles
2 to 4 strawberry jam or grape jelly packets

Wrap waffles in tin foil and place on manifold. Remove toasted waffles after 100 miles, and top with butter and jelly packages.

Wide Load Waffles
Breakfast Pastry

Prepackaged biscuits
Butter
Cinnamon
Sugar
Brown sugar

Coat the bottom and edges of a rectangular tin pan generously with cooking spray. Roll biscuits flat using full soda pop can, then press and form the dough to line bottom of pan. Drizzle with melted butter. Shake together cinnamon and sugars and sprinkle on top. Bake 2 hours at 55 mph.

Dumplings

Serve these with Chicken and Dumplings recipe found on page 47.

½ cup flour
½ cup cornmeal
1 teaspoon baking powder
Freshly chopped thyme (like you have a lot of this laying around, right?)
½ cup milk
2 tablespoons oil
Pinch of salt

Combine above ingredients in a plastic bowl and stir just until moistened. Drop by spoonfuls onto chicken stew, recover with foil, and set back on manifold. Drive 150 miles to cook and brown dumplings, then serve yourself up a healthy portion of this mouth-watering dish.

Chapter 9
Sauces and Soda Can Sauces

Soda can sauces are both fun and creative. Since you'll probably find yourself making them on a very regular basis, buy the generic soda pop brands available at most grocery stores for as little as .97 cents a six pack.

BBQ Sauce
long version

    1 can open cola
    ½ small onion, chopped
    6 packets catsup
    2 packets mustard
    1 spoonful extra dark molasses
    1 spoonful vinegar

Open one can of cola. Cover with foil and simmer on idle overnight (10 hours).

Pour off ¼ of overnight heated cola, and add above ingredients. Cover with foil and return to manifold. Cook for 450 miles at 65 mph, swirling once after 200 miles.

Economy BBQ Sauce

½ can of cola
1 package chopped onions
6 packets catsup
2 packets mustard
½ packet sugar
Salt and pepper

Pour all ingredients into cola can. Cover with foil and set securely on manifold, making sure to avoid contact with turbo. Cook for 450 miles at 65 mph, swirling once after 200 miles.

Mop Sauce in a Soda Can

½ cup water
¼ cup vinegar
½ cup Worcestershire sauce
¼ cup ketchup
¼ cup dark corn syrup
2 tablespoons oil
2 tablespoons mustard
2 teaspoons instant-coffee granules
1 teaspoon salt and pepper
¼ teaspoon Tabasco sauce

Pour all ingredients in a soda can, cover, and simmer for anywhere up to 300 miles. You can pour this sauce over any type of beef for basting, cooking, or glazing. It is especially good basted over a beef brisket.

Smillin' Cec's Chunky BBQ Sauce

1 cup catsup
Chunk-size pieces of fresh tomatoes and onions
8 ounce can of pineapple chunks
Worchester sauce
Soy sauce
Malt vinegar
Dry mustard
Seasoning salt

Place all ingredients into tin pan. Cover with foil and set securely on manifold. Cook for 220 miles; driving speed is not a factor in cooking chunky BBQ sauce.

Many Ingredient BBQ Sauce

This sauce may have too many items for you to have on board your rig. It's included because it is so dang good, and an age-old family recipe from Great Great Grandma Jorgensen. If you can get your hands on everything needed, it is worth making a double or triple batch.

1 tablespoon olive oil
1 chopped jumbo onion
2 tablespoons chopped, peeled, fresh ginger
2 tablespoons chili powder
3 crushed garlic cloves
1 can crushed pineapple in juice
1 can crushed tomatoes in puree
½ cup ketchup
¼ cup vinegar
3 tablespoons brown sugar
3 tablespoons molasses
2 teaspoons dry mustard
1 teaspoon salt

Pour all ingredients into deep tin pan. Mix and mash together well to break down tomatoes. Cover partially with foil and set securely on manifold. This sauce is best when cooked at slower speeds and a lower rpm for a distance of 175-225 miles. Avoid steep grades and turns to avoid spillage.

If you don't use all the BBQ sauce right away, it'll stay fresh in an ice cooler for up to 1 week. If you have any home-time scheduled, you can swing by and store it in your freezer for up to two months.

Homemade Tomato Sauce

You'll want to make a big match of this tomato sauce, and store it in separate containers in your ice chest or refrigerator to use with a whole host of recipes in this cookbook.

> 2 cans (16-ounce) tomato sauce
> 1 8-ounce can tomato paste
> Onion
> Garlic
> Pepperoni slices (chopped)
> Oregano
> Italian seasoning salt

The night before, chop one small onion. Peel two cloves of garlic, and seal with chopped onion in a tightly wrapped package of aluminum foil. Place the pouch on a preheated manifold and idle at 300 rpm for 8 to 9 hours.

In a tin container, combine all above ingredients. Cover and bake at 55 mph for 4 to 5 hours. Stir, recover, and bake an additional 4 hours.

Chinese Sparerib Sauce

2 tablespoons oil
2 sliced green onions
½ cup brown sugar
4 packages soy sauce
¼ cup cooking sherry
1 tablespoon corn starch
1 teaspoon ginger

Place all ingredients in can or tin container, and cover with foil before placing on manifold. Since you cannot overcook Chinese sparerib sauce, remove it whenever convenient throughout your day's drive. Use this sauce to spoon over pork spareribs, pork chops, or chicken or turkey parts before cooking meat dish on your engine.

Teriyaki Sauce

2 packets of soy sauce
1 ginger root
Canned pineapples
2 spoonfuls of red wine vinegar
1 packet of mustard
Glove of minced garlic
Cloves

Cut ginger root small enough to fit into the opening of a cleaned soda can. Add remaining ingredients, cover with foil, and simmer overnight. Then, bake the sauce for 500 miles at 55 to 65 mph.

Any Town Brown Gravy

1 package brown gravy mix
Onions
Mushrooms
Meat drippings
Cornstarch
Water

Mix above ingredients and place into soda can. Heat thoroughly driving at least 150 miles.

Mississippi Mud Sauce

This sauce should look like the Mississippi river as you drive I-40 West across the Arkansas state line.

Leftover drippings from manifold meat dish
Brown gravy (page 83)
Two packages chopped onions
Two packages relish
Tabasco hot sauce

Place all ingredients in a soda can, and cook on manifold for 325 miles. Pour the Mississippi mud sauce liberally over any meat dish of your choosing.

Arizona Red Soda Can Sauce

One red bell pepper
Hot peppers
One whole fresh tomato

Chop everything to fit into soda can, seeds and all. Cook on manifold across Arizona into New Mexico.

Soda Can Garlic and Onion Spread

This trucker's favorite is good on chips, bread, or just about anything you can find to spread it on!

> 2 cloves garlic
> Chopped onions
> Butter

After peeling the garlic cloves, place above ingredients in a clean soda can. Cover tightly with foil, and bake on the manifold for 400 miles at any rate of speed. As this one cooks (assuming you're a garlic fan), it is well worth opening your tractor's fresh air intake vents to catch a whiff every now and again.

After carefully removing the foil top from the can, use a fork or spoon to mash the ingredients together and break up the roasted garlic cloves.

Key West Lemon Lime Dipping Sauce

Perfect for chicken nuggets!

½ can lemon lime soda
1 lemon picked fresh off a Florida lemon tree
1 packet sugar
1 spoonful pectin

Wash the lemon fruit and cut in half. Squeeze the juice into a soda can. Scoop out the lemon pulp from the shell and cover the soda can top with the lemon shell. Cover the can with foil and bake for 400 miles. Pour the sauce into another clean soda container and let cool and thicken before serving.

Tex-Mex Border Sauce

If you've acquired the taste for spicy Mexican dishes along the Southern border states, try this sauce to add fire to any meal.

> Leftover drippings from manifold meat dish
> ½ can refried beans
> Red kidney beans
> Chunks of chopped tomatoes and onions
> Bell pepper slices
> Jalapeno chilies
> Red chilies (seeds removed)
> Tabasco (use as much as you can stand)

Mash all ingredients together in a tin pan, cover tightly with foil and cook on manifold for 325 miles.

Chapter 10
Hors d'oeuvres and Snacks

Easy to make snacks that are as good as any restaurant can offer.

Construction Zone Calzones

1 can Pillsbury refrigerated biscuits
Mushrooms
Cheese
1 packet ketchup
Splash of mountain water
Dash Italian seasoning

Chop the mushroom and shred the cheese. Include chopped onions if your mouth is watering for them. Roll the biscuits out flat, combine all the above ingredients and layer on dough, then roll out to whatever size you see fit. Seal the edges with the tin of a fork, making it look real fancy like!

Wrap in foil and place on manifold for 300 miles.

Peterbuilt Pizzas

Whether your name is Peter or not, you can build your own pizza and cook it to order right under the hood.

> 1 can Pillsbury refrigerated biscuits
> Can of tomato sauce
> Parsley
> Mozzarella cheese packets
> Pizza toppings (meat, mushrooms, onions, olives, old shoes, etc.)

Roll the biscuits out flat to create a round or rectangular pizza, pour on the tomato sauce, and build whatever type of pizza you're craving. Top with cheese and chopped parsley. Lay onto appropriate size cooking pan, cover with foil, and bake on the manifold for 300 miles.

Nogales Nachos

This is a dish to write home about. It smells delicious, and tastes even better.

> 1-ounce bag tortilla chips
> 1-ounce bag Frito corn chips
> 1 very small onion
> 1 jalapeno pepper
> 1 can refried beans
> Chopped olives
> Shredded cheese

Coat a tin pan with cooking spray. Layer corn and tortilla chips in pan, and sprinkle with cheese. Cover tin pan tightly with foil.

Pack and mix the refried beans, onion, jalapeno, and olives into a clean tuna can. Wrap can tightly with foil.

Heat both containers on manifold for 250 miles at 55 to 65 mph. When serving, add chopped tomatoes and sour cream if desired.

Refried Bean Dip

One can of pork and beans (or prepared refried
    bean dip)
Jalapeno peppers
Red chilies
Green chilies
Salt and pepper to taste

Drain sauce from can of pork and beans and rinse with water.
Depending on your palette (or how many miles you plan to
drive after eating this concoction), slow roast the above ingredients in their original can for 200 miles. After the first 100
miles, toss on some tortilla chips wrapped in foil and a hot,
crispy dipping snack.

Southern Alabama Slow Roasted Salted Peanuts

Raw peanuts
20 packets of salt from a fast food restaurant

Soak raw peanuts in one pound empty coffee can overnight in heavy salt water. Drain (do not rinse) and cover coffee can tightly with tin foil the next morning, and pierce a few small holes for the steam to escape before placing on manifold. Tumble every 150 miles for 600 miles.

Truckers Trail Mix

Another recipe that deviates from the theme of this cookbook, but included because it is so apropos for our reading audience.

You old timers remember this time-honored concoction under a different name: Gorp. Whatever you call it, this midday snack helps satisfy your craving and quiet the rumblin' complaints from your stomach as you smell your hot roast beef, potato, and onion dinner cooking ever so fragrant through the tractor's fresh air intake vents.

> Salted brown peanuts or variety of mixed nuts
> Cashew pieces
> Crushed vanilla wafers
> M & Ms
> Raisins
> Coconut flakes
> Dried fruit pieces (such as apples, bananas, cherries, and apricots)

Place all ingredients in a very large Tupperware-type container. Cover tightly (for storage and freshness) and shake to mix. Making a colossal batch of trail mix is recommended to last you hundreds of miles and days driving down the endless black ribbon.

Dole yourself out portions of gorp to stave the munchies monster. It's best to grab a handful and toss it into a plastic sack with the ends rolled over. Then, mold and nestle the contents like a bean bag into the crook of your dash and windshield well within arm's reach to avoid any spilling or mess on the carpet or driver's seat. As Grandma Jorgensen always says, cleanliness is next to Godliness!

Chapter 11
Adding Some Spice to Your Life

You can find a whole variety of spices that you can pick fresh right along the side of the road. Some farmers even list the crops they grow, and what you can help yourself to in a bounty harvest. Always ask permission first from Joe Farmer before galloping through his field, and reward him in turn with a hot roll slathered in roasted garlic and onion spread. You'll sure to have made a new friend for life!

Pippy Longstocking Stuffing

Joyce Jorgensen, late wife of Cecil Jorgensen, was easily recognized at truck stops and loading docks across the country wearing her signature Daisy Doo floppy black hat and long blonde braids. When not driving her tiny red convertible Miata (with license plate holder, "My other car is an 18-wheeler"), or riding shotgun on the semi with Cecil, writing or crocheting, Joyce enjoyed laying on the beach and playing in the warm ocean waters along the south eastern gulf of Mexico.

Joyce also enjoyed cooking, and this stuffing concoction was one of her personal favorites.

Day old (plus) bag of bread crumbs
Small onion
Celery
Mushrooms
Crushed walnuts
Raisins (optional, but good)
Crème of mushroom soup
Chicken bouillon cube
Onion salt

Dissolve the bouillon cube in a coffee can filled 2/3rds with hot water. Add dried breadcrumbs to the water mixture, and mash with any utensil to break the hard bread apart.

Chop the onion, celery, and mushrooms into random large pieces (don't dice too fine, or you'll destroy the flavor). Add the vegetables, walnuts, crème of mushroom soup (saving the can!), and salt to the coffee can. Top with a generous dollop of butter, and cover tightly with foil. Cook on the manifold for 450 miles, the equivalents of one day's worth of crocheting. Serve with any of the poultry or meat dishes found in this cookbook.

Tip: *You can buy a large bag of one, two, or three-day-old bread-crumbs from any commercial supermarket that has a bakery department. If they don't give it to you for free, you'll at most pay .50 cents or so for the entire bag.*

Chapter 12
Desserts

Diesel S'Mores

It's impossible to buy Girl Scout cookies on the road from a semi truck. Support the troops in spirit by enjoying this traditional favorite snack of scouts and campers alike.

Graham crackers
Marshmallows
Chocolate candy bar

Roast marshmallows on a stick over open campfire or cooling diesel engine. Slide toasted marshmallow between two graham crackers wedged with chocolate square.

Polar Eskimo Pies

You could satisfy your sweet tooth and craving for something sweet after dinner by just buying an over priced candy bar from a truck stop. Or, you can make your own Eskimo pies for a fraction of the cost, and they taste better, too.

Graham crackers
Chocolate Hershey candy bar
Vanilla ice cream

The last 100 miles of your driving day, wrap graham crackers in foil and place on manifold. When you're ready for dessert, take warmed crackers and sandwich ice cream and chocolate between them (the hot crackers lightly melts the flavor of the chocolate and ice cream together).

Food Tip: Buy ice cream packaged in rectangular shaped cartons. It's easy to peel back the carton and slice off a perfectly shaped slab of ice cream to fit in these Eskimo pie sandwiches.

Phyllo Strudel

4 sheets phyllo
Apples
Cinnamon
Sugar drizzle mixture

Stack phyllo sheets together. Brush the top sheet with butter. Cut phylllo into square.

Wenatchee Applesauce

3 to 4 peeled apples
½ cup brown sugar
¾ cup water
½ teaspoon cinnamon
½ teaspoon nutmeg
Pinch of salt

Core the peeled apples, and chop into pieces (what size is not important). Combine with remaining ingredients in tin pan, cover, and place on manifold. After driving 400 miles, remove and mash to create a large bowlful of applesauce. Crumble some brown sugar on top of your serving to really bring out and enhance the flavor of the baked in cinnamon.

If you are accustomed to eating pink applesauce, leave the skins on the apples as they cook under the hood. Then, simply peel back and remove the cooked skins

Food tip: *The best apples for applesauce are McIntosh, Granny Smith, and Romes to name a few. Avoid apples like Red or Golden Delicious because they tend to be grainy after cooking. If you're driving through Wenatchee, Washington in the summer time, pick up an entire crate of fresh apples. That, and Walla Walla onions from Washington, are indigenous to the great northwest and always worth making room for on board to enhance your diesel dining experience.*

Chapter 13
Liquid Refreshments

Cowboy Coffee

Drinking coffee and ingesting small amounts of caffeine through-out the day is medically proven to be more effective in keeping you alert than slugging down 2-3 cups before you start your day's drive. Using this recipe, keeping the grounds in the blend acts as a deterrent from gulping the coffee too quickly.

And for you old-school truckers, this is the only legal method as of the printing of this cookbook to keep you awake and help you to stay between the white lines on those long night hauls.

This is a recipe resurrected from the days of the Old West.

> Two scoops of ground (or crushed) coffee
> Fresh water

Place the coffee into a filter, and secure and lower the filter into a 1 pound tin can of water. Place on the manifold and idle overnight at 1000 rpm. Strain the brew into a coffee cup by pouring slowly though a coffee filter or paper towel.

Warning: This is stronger than any cup of coffee you have ever purchased at a truck stop or fancy coffee latte stand. Be forewarned to its effects!

Cigarette Coffee

There are still some truckers out there who steadfastly refuse to give up on one last vice: cigarettes. While it's a nasty habit, it ain't illegal yet. Try this recipe to get a real nicotine jolt!

> One scoop (cup) of your favorite coffee blend
> Loose tobacco
> Fresh water

Place the coffee grounds and tobacco shavings in a filter, and secure and lower the filter into a tin can of water. Place on the manifold and idle overnight at 1000 rpm.

West Coast Turnaround Tea

This recipe extracts every drop of caffeine from your tea bags and the coffee grounds, and tastes just as strong as it is. However the results from its effects are the next best thing to having a second driver on board.

Tea bags
Coffee grounds

Add five tea bags to a one pound coffee can filled with water. Pour in ¼ cup of coffee grounds, cover with foil, and cook on the manifold all day.

Strain the brewed tea mixture into a coffee cup by pouring slowly though a coffee filter or paper towel. Consume as needed throughout the night.

Long Island Ice Tea

Use the extra pay you receive as a company driver for driving through Long Island to treat yourself to a good dinner (see page 28 for the recipe on Beef Tenderloin) and this fancy beverage.

Sun tea
Lemons
Marichino cherries
Optional ingredients for home-time consumption

Make a strong batch of brewed tea, and place the sealed container somewhere in your tractor that gets sunlight (try the dashboard this doesn't block your driving vision).

Uphill Grade Trucker Gatorade
Florida Alligatorade

Wal-Mart cherry drink mix, pre-sweetened
Orange slices
Cold water

Mix water and cherry drink mix in a covered, tall Pilot Tanker cup, and give it a good shake. Add some ice cubes and orange slices to enjoy a cold drink that'll really quench your thirst. (If you make this mix at home, and don't have to drive any type of vehicle, add some Vodka to the juice for a real pick-me-up.)

Martha Stewart Prison Bowl Punch

The Queen of Clean and Cooking is sporting designer jump-suit stripes after her guilty verdict on tax evasion. But as long as she keeps her commode sparklin' fresh and sani white, it could be used as a punch bowl for those prison parties and social inmate get togethers!

> Two cups fruit punch
> 1 liter bottle of lemon-lime soda pop
> Orange slices
> Ice cubes

Combine above ingredients in large plastic container with a lid. When you're ready to feast upon your diesel dining home cooked meal, give the container a good shake and pour yourself a refreshing cool drink to accompany your meal and quench your thirst.

Chapter 14
Meal Planning

Hearty Meals

Nothings tastes better than meat and potatoes cooked on a diesel engine.

Eating and Living Well

Part of a healthy diet depends on both eating and living well. Consider the following salt-of-the-earth advise from 87-year old Grandma Jorgensen:

A man should work hard and earn an honest living; idle time is the devil's workshop. Use both your muscles and your mind.

Eat a well balanced meals containing the four basic food groups. Don't folly or pay attention to any type of fad diets. According to Grandma, when she hears "Low carb" she retorts, "a carburetor belongs in an automobile."

Treat others as you would want others to treat you.

Get plenty of rest, stay in close contact with family, and be kind and loving to your family and friends

Exercise is important, too. Reserve the spare tire for your blown out retreads. Use your mandatory pre-vehicle inspection to also stretch and limber for the day. Reach and stretch high as you pull open the hood of your tractor. Bend at the waist examining the front suspension, and stoop and look for any obvious leaks from underneath your rig. Use a lunging, almost dance-like stretch when checking your brake hubs and pads. When done properly, this simple workout will keep you trim, tone, fit, and alert as you start the day's drive. Then, pour yourself a cup of Cowboy Coffee (page 103), grab a breakfast sandwich (page 72) from the manifold, and hit the road!

Maintain your health: there is nothing worse than driving a truck for 11 hours a day when you're feeling anything other than in stellar health. See page 85 for some suggestions on how you can be feeling better in a jiffy.

Tools and Essentials

- With just a few basic items, you can eat home-style meals that are hot, healthy, and wholesome. Before you start your Diesel Dining cooking experience, you should have on board the following basic tools and supplies:
- Plastic silverware, paper plates, and paper towels
- One sharp kitchen knife
- Meat thermometer
- Hot gloves for oven mitts
- Potato and vegetable peeler, and brush to clean
- Cheese shredder
- Cutting board (white plastic for hygienic purposes: not wooden)
- Good quality aluminum foil (high quality foil, while it might cost a few cents more, is worth it to prevents leaks and spillage on the manifold)
- Cast iron pan with handle (save money and buy cast iron cookware at a thrift shop)
- Foil cooking pans (often available in packs of three for under $1)
- Clean tin cans in a variety of sizes (soup cans should be 10 ounces)
- Soda cans for sauces; see page 85
- One pound and three pound size empty coffee cans
- Potatoes and onions storage bags (netted, or a knotted nylon stocking).

Tip: Wrap bulk vegetables loosely in newspaper and store in a cardboard box for freshness. This is an especially good method for keeping potatoes from spoiling.

- T.V. tray (collapsible, to fold up for storage)
- Cooking spray, butter, lard, and beef suet

Condiments available for free in one-pack servings from all fast food restaurants and truck stops (such as catsup, mustard, soy sauce, relish, chopped onions, lemon juice, honey, Parmesan cheese packages, salt, and pepper). Of course, helping yourself to these condiments assumes that you make a purchase from the establishment.

It's handy to have any the following items available: Flour, corn starch, spices (such as seasoning salt, garlic salt, coarse ground pepper, parsley, oregano flakes, basil, chili powder), creamed soups (mushroom or chicken), canned tomato sauce, Tabasco and Worchester sauce, vinegar, quick cooking rice and noodles, packaged gravy, bullion cubes (beef and chicken), bread crumbs, corn flakes, milk, cheese, sugar, cinnamon, and marshmallows

Liquid smoke, if you plan to barbecue meat to accompany a diesel-cooked side dish

You can easily keep all your supplies handy and in one location in the sidebox of your tractor. This storage area can also be used to house an inexpensive barbecue, which enhances and adds greater variety to your diesel dining dishes, and a couple of comfortable lawn chairs that collapse umbrella-like into nylon bags (a very inexpensive, yet worthwhile, purchase at Wal-Mart or Kmart stores). For additional storage, try strapping a plastic milk crate to the catwalk and using this area to store items such as briquettes, spray cleaner, and the like.

By definition, a pinch of salt is that which you can pick up with your thumb and index finger. A punch of salt is a fistful. A plastic spoon for Wendy's holds exactly 1 ½ a teaspoon.

Cooking Times

For all meat recipes in this cookbook, be sure to use a meat thermometer to check for doneness. For example with beef:

Medium rare: 150°F

Medium: 160°F

Well done: 170°F

Poultry and pork are typically cooked to a temperature of 170°F.

A good rule of thumb for checking the doneness of meat is when it is, "fork tender." Also, when cooking chicken, you know it is done when the juices run clear.

Warning: It is strongly recommended that you not consume meat cooked rare (below 150°F), to avoid any bacteria-related contamination.

All cooking times listed in this cookbook are based on 60 mph unless otherwise noted. Make adjustments and add time for altitude changes, road construction, traffic, and other weather-related slow downs.

Cooking temperatures and times also vary based on your differential, and the legal speed for trucks state-to-state. For example, you'll cook your stew a lot faster driving across Utah (up to 75 mph, depending on your carrier) than you will California (55 mph).

Baking definitions for truck driving chef:

Slow bake: 55 mph

Hot bake: 6% upgrade

In the box: Load weight in trailer

Tenderizing Meat

Since the author's of this cookbook always have your bottom line dollar in mind, we encourage buying and using the most inexpensive cuts of meat available. We are able to get away with such shameless brashness not to suggest that you deprive yourself from eating the more expensive cuts of beef, but rather spending that money unnecessarily is simply a waste of your cents earned per mile. Your diesel engine already does such an efficient job in tenderizing even the toughest cut of meat, just like a pressure cooker would do on your traditional stove at home.

In our vast travels, we have discovered that a stereotypical trait of many trucker drivers is that of an obsessive-compulsive nature. This includes both cleanliness (due mostly in part to the lack of control of constant dirt and dust entering and swirling about the inside of your tractor) and might also apply to your eating habits.

If you feel the need to tenderize any cuts of meat when using the recipes from this book, try the following method that also allows you to vent any pent up frustration and tension you might still be feeling at the end of a very long day of driving:

Wrap the meat in a plastic bag, then re-wrap the entire package in a full newspaper.

Lay the package on the ground, and beat upon it with your Tire Billie or king pin puller.

Whacking on the meat breaks down the tougher cuts of gristle, and leaves you with a restaurant-style piece of beef.

Beef Cuts

Ever stand there scratching your head at the meat counter, trying to remember which type of meat you need for a particular recipe? Wonder no more; tuck this cookbook into your back pocket, and use it as a reference guide when shopping for beef. All cuts of beef can be cooked on your manifold: the parenthetical cooking methods are more traditional so you can also use this information away from your place of business.

- Beef rib roast small end (roast). Also called standing rib roast.
- Beef rib-eye roast (roast). Large center muscle of rib with bones and seam fat removed.

- Beef bottom round cut (braise, roast). Also called beef bottom round pot roast.
- Beef chuck boneless shoulder pot roast (braise). Also called English or cross rib roast.
- Beef chuck 7-bone steak (braise). Named for bone that looks like the number 7; also called center chuck steak.
- Beef chuck short ribs (braise, cook in liquid). Also called barbecue ribs.
- Beef shank cross cuts (braise, cook in liquid). Crosswise cuts from foreshank or hindshank.
- Beef top loin steak (broil, grill, panbroil, panfry).
- Beef loin porterhouse steak (broil, grill, panbroil, panfry). Includes at least 1¼ inches diameter of tenderloin.
- Beef rib-eye steak (broil, grill, panbroil, panfry). Also called fillet steak; cut from beef rib-eye roast.
- Beef top round steak (broil, grill, panbroil).
- Beef loin tenderloin roast (roast, grill, broil). Cut from tenderloin muscle; very tender, boneless, with little if any fat covering. This tender cut of beef tapers from a broad butt end to a narrower, thinner tip. To roast it whole, tuck the narrow end under to make the meat look uniformly thick.
- Chateaubriand, the first cut after removing the butt of the beef tenderloin, is a cut about 2 to 3 inches long.
- Tournedos are filet steaks, cut from the center of a beef tenderloin into about 1-inch thick slices.
- Filet mignon, a small cut of beef close to the narrow end of the tenderloin, is cut into about 1-inch thick slices.

Bobtail Shopping

When you're not hauling around an extra 53 feet of trailer, take advantage of your sporty Bobtail and stock up on food supplies. Frequent locations that would not otherwise be available to you.

And take advantage of all free stuff! Plastic utensils are available at all restaurants, and you drive by enough open fields down the interstates to know where you can safely pull off and help yourself to some fresh vegetables (be sure to ask the farmer, first— you don't need a backside blister of rock salt from an angry farmer).

Chapter 15
Diesel Dining Tips and Tricks

People *not in the know* have the misconception that truck stop coffee shops and restaurants have the best food because they always see a host of rigs parked outside. Eating where you can easily and conveniently park your truck indicates that the food is probably both overpriced and greasy. Bring your diesel-cooked dinner with you, instead, to a relaxing rest area with a mountainous view. Plus, soothing and tranquil surroundings are good for digestion.

Using Free Library Services in Any Town

Libraries offer a lot more than people realize other than checking out books and magazines for a couple of weeks. These extra perks are appreciated most and especially useful for long-haul truck drivers.

At the library you have both a computer and printer at your fingertips. This gives you free Internet access (to check email, for example), and lets you print important mail and other documents. You can also use your email account to simulate information you otherwise would need to fax to someone. Simply email the document as an attached file to yourself in an email; you can then open and forward the file as needed whenever you're at a local library.

Plus, surrounding yourself amongst well-read, articulate people will ground you back to the human race. Seeing other adults immersed in books and reference materials, exercising their intellect instead of performing blue collar labor tasks, draws you out of the trance inevitably brought on by the endless hours of driving. A helpful and necessary reminder that the world doesn't revolve around truck stops and engaging in mindless conversation about the last Jerry Springer episode.

Finally, spending a two hour break outside the truck and immersing yourself in a quiet, non-vibrating environment, is a refreshing and probably much needed break from those long hours of driving

How Having a Cell Phone Pays for Itself

Okay, you're one of the last holdouts … you have refused to ever buy a cell phone. Plus, it's against most company policy and some state laws to talk on the cell phone in a vehicle anyway. But by having a cell phone on board, and purchasing the correct calling plan, you actually wind up saving money (and time) in the short run and long haul.

If you're a company driver, take the example of calling into one of their many departments. Logs or payroll, for example. How long do you spend on hold waiting for the Musak to be replaced with a human voice? Minutes? ½ hour? 45 minutes to one hour? Time is money, and you're not making a dime when your wheels are not turning. Sitting on hold at a pay phone in a truck stop is not only a waste of time, but just for chuckles consider the appeal of the stress reduction when you are almost inevitably cutoff or disconnected after investing 30 minutes of your time on hold.

If you have a cell phone on board, a) you don't have to pull over and find a pay phone, b) you can use the ear piece to keep your hands free for driving as you wait on hold, and c) you won't pay any additional phone charges since the calling plan you purchased takes into account that you are a long-haul trucker and you can therefore use your phone from anywhere in the United States.

Having a cell phone is also a time saver, and stress reducer, when you need to call the consignee to either confirm an appointment time or get accurate directions.

Finally, Ma Bell has never waived in her message that the phone gives you immediate access to family and loved ones whenever you want to pick it up and press the speed dial button. And the reverse also holds true; there would be no other way for someone to contact you since you are literally on the move 100% of the time.

Chapter 16
Trucker Ramblings

Smillin' Cec's Corner

This section contains no holds barred opinions from Cecil, the truck driver and licensed CDL carrying author. His handle throughout life has always been *Smillin' Cec*, as he Cheshire's his signature grin. In his trademark baritone *made for radio* voice, Cecil unabashedly shares with friends his uncensored perceptions riddled with good humor and wit. Next time you see Smillin' Cec cruising down the interstate in his semi, give him the double-toot arm signal and he'll reward you with a trademark smile and blast from the air horn!

You are what you eat: stop giving your money away to the franchise junk food conglomerates

After being on the road, driving for 11 hours that have extended to 14 because of sitting at a loading dock for 3 ½ hours, my reward had been a slimy hot dog on a stale bun. Sold to me by a rude, over-worked convenience store clerk. As I sit here alone in the sweltering heat in this no idling law state gnawing on my weenie dinner, I am lonely, tired, and hungry: $1.99 slimy wiener dog. $1.49 cup of soda pop. Throw in the sales tax for a state I don't even live in, and that's around $3.77 for a meal that only satisfies my hunger need for around half an hour, then leaves my stomach churning and festering the remainder of the night. While I may not hold a Masters Degree, I am a qualified graduate from the School of Hard Knocks. There is something seriously wrong with this picture.

Enter the alternative. A satisfying, fulfilling meal of roast beef, potatoes, carrots, gravy, home made bread and dessert for less than half the price. Read this cookbook. Follow its recipes. You'll save a ton of money, frustration, and stomach ulcers. And you'll also have the satisfaction of not lining the pockets of the Cash Cow Enterprises that take trucker's hard-earned money for cheap, lousy food product!

How I feel about junk food vs. home cooked food

For some reason, 4-wheelers assume that if a restaurant has a lot of semis parked around it, that the food has to be good. As professional drivers, we know that myth has long since died with the original owners, who knew us by our first names and always asked about the family back home. Unfortunately, these honest, hard working old time entrepreneurs have been replaced by every short order sleaze ball franchise on the planet. I miss the humanity, common courtesy, and respect that was buried and lost so long ago.

One thing I have not been logically able to figure out is how a restaurant can sell me a .99 cent all beef burger? I know for a fact that ground round at the time of this writing is $3.49 a pound from the meat counter. Are the franchises so large that they can purchase ground round at lower prices than my mega store sells it to me raw?

We all know what goes into hot dogs and baloney (whether we'll admit it or not), but have you ever thought about the hamburger you're chowing down? Their only way to provide you with this delicacy they refer to as "lunch" is include every cow, steer, bull, and milk cow body part that can be ground and passed as beef.

Don't forget that truck drivers are human, too

Take the time to tell your dispatcher you need a break to remind yourself that you're a member of the human race. "The freight can wait: I'm the most important cargo on this truck!"

"Okay, so I'm a neat freak who happens to drive a truck"

Keep in mind the stereotypical appearance of the people working at truck stops. Rude people don't have time to offer a pleasant smile ... etc., do you think they care about their hygiene or your personal health while they handle and prepare your food? The sign posted in the restrooms is not an ironclad guarantee that a disgruntled worker is going to surgically scrub his hands before leaving the urinal.

Cleanliness: to make a sanitizing solution (because you have raw meat on truck), use two or three tablespoons of bleach to a gallon of water. Guaranteed to kill all bacteria. Living on this truck presents its own host of clean problems. When you add to that mix home style baking, it compounds the problem. The solution to keeping everything sanitized is rinsing dishes and cleaning surfaces with a mixture of water and bleach.

How I deal with non-English speaking dock workers

We've all been frustrated on loading docks, especially close to the Mexico border where workers [seemingly] cannot understand English. Do you ever question whether they truly don't understand, or perhaps are just playing with you adding a level of frustration to your job that is already filled with deadlines and stress?

To countermand this situation, you can start speaking to them in another foreign language you're familiar with. If you're not multi-lingual, make something up–even Pig Latin will do! Or simply play stupid: their goal is to get the signed BOL to transport the goods across the border. You'll be pleasantly surprised to see how quickly the English language becomes part of their mother tongue. You can bet your fifth wheel that they'll understand these very basic phrases:

- Where is the loading dock?
- Which dock number do I want?
- Bathroom?
- Sign the BOL, por favor. (At least you can leave on a pleasant note by closing with a Spanish nicety!)
- Of course if they keep you waiting too long, you can take advantage of this time to prepare a meal from this book. (Which you don't have to share—your payback is to torture the obstinate workers with the home cooked smells of diesel dining!)

My advice for new (wet behind the ears) truck drivers

If you're pulled over by a Smokey and haven't been speeding, and the lawman's excuse is vague or rhetorical, such as you "might have drifted over the fog line," chances are you look suspicious. Shaggy hair and an unkempt appearance not only reflect poorly on the reputation of the company that employs you, but also could be detrimental to you in the long run. You want to avoid a ticket or a potential log violation at all costs: the fees imposed on truckers are stiff, high, unwavering, and come directly out of your pocket. And remember, your CDL is your license to the highway. If you lose that, you'll be back to flipping burgers at the local fast food joint.

While I'm not telling young truckers to sell out and join the Establishment, at least put on a clean shirt and look willing.

Just Say No

Your job is important to you: ethically, morally, and financially. But when you're asked (pressured?) to drive through dangerous conditions under forced dispatch to deliver a load, JUST SAY NO. Not only do you put yourself at risk, but also endanger the lives of everyone else on the road.

First, ask yourself what you are hauling. Is your life worth timely delivery of a semi-full of toilet tissue to a distribution center in New England in the dead of night during a winter storm? Of course it is your responsibility as a truck driver to deliver the load on time. But always remember (and this is easy to forget when you're fatigued and under pressure), let common sense prevail. It's your life and livelihood in exchange for a load of merchandise.

Work with your dispatcher in these rare situations, and you'll always arrive alive. If you cannot negotiate or reason with your dispatcher, understand that he or she values the load more than you or your family.

Feeling Sick? Old Trucker Onboard Remedies

Driving when you are ailing is less than fun, and distorts your concentration when all your mind can focus on are your body's aches and pains. Try taking advantage of these simple, old school remedies:

- For muscle relief, use one of those disposable hot pads.
- For cold relief, make some mint tea.
- Sagebrush tea works great when gout flares up.

Road Kill: Not Too Appetizing a Topic

Road kill should obviously be left to the clean up of the professional, state-paid, highway workers. However, if you're a hunter, you might find one exception to this rule ....

There is absolutely no reason to waste good deer meat. If Bambi accidentally gallops in front of your high beams and you are unable to avoid contact, the best part of meat on a deer is the 2-inch by 6-inch long strip along the back. Cook this delicacy as you would any other piece of fine meat on your manifold—sealed tightly in a foil pan for 600 miles.

Closing Thoughts

Working, living, and eating in an 8-foot by 10-foot space of a tractor pulling semi truck trailers across the country is challenging in itself. Because of the recessive economy that arose from the late 1990s, Cecil revocated from maintenance electrician to truck driver to ensure future job security in an uncertain and lackluster job market. His late wife, Joyce, put a long-term technical writing career on hold to ride shotgun. Together, they worked (i.e., were responsible and on call) 24 hours a day, seven days a week. Cumulatively, they earned less than one third of what they were making in their previous professions. Money made delivering loads was a hard-earned commodity, and the flavor of a home cooked meal more appreciated than ever.

In the true survival spirit of trucking and a sign of our economic status and staunch conservatism, this cookbook was written on an eight-year-old Toshiba laptop donated by a relative. Just as we seemed to do on a daily basis, the laptop took a beating as the potholes and road construction ruts on America's freeway system tossed and jostled everything inside the cab. The computer display crystal cracked halfway through writing this book when it fell crossing a particularly bumpy area in Southern Utah. This reduced the screen real estate by around 40%; another challenge to overcome.

Persistence and tenacity often come with a price tag, and the end result with the publishing of this cookbook was well worth the inconvenience of its inception and creation. While the writing, stories, and recipe names are entertaining, the intent of this book is to teach you how to cook nourishing, hearty, and affordable meals using your semi truck's diesel engine.

You already take the time each day to perform your rig's mandatory pre and post-trip DOT inspection, routinely check the oil levels, ensure all engine maintenance work is performed, and fuel the tanks daily. You should be performing this same routine on its driver—you! The end result to any form of wholesome eating is a healthy body, mind, and soul.

NOTES